Sensational Sensibilities

Understanding your Super Senses

Sensational Sensibilities
Understanding your Super Senses

Patricia Farrenkopf, Ed.D

Owner and Creator of

PGi TM
ProGift-ify

Fishtail Publishing

Book designed by Erin O'Neil
www.erinoneil.org

Cover image by Karlis Reimanis on Unsplash
Cover design by Erin O'Neil

Published in the USA by Fishtail Publishing LLC
Westerville, OH

www.fishtailpublishing.org

ISBN: 978-1-7333380-2-8
LCCN: 2020918451

To all the gifted individuals whose
asynchronous development and intensities
make them fascinating!

We Are the Music Makers

We are the music makers,
And we are the dreamers of dreams...
Yet we are the movers and shakers
Of the world for ever, it seems.

Arthur William Edgar O'Shaughnessy

Table of Contents

Acknowledgments

Many thanks to Amber Nickels, Holly Kramer, Deb Logan, Diane McClaskey, Valerie Jasinski, Rachel Dobney, and K.Dana Kagrise. Your reviews of my educational tool card game and book have made all the difference.

Introduction

I have been learning about, working with, and teaching educators about gifted and high ability learners for most of my career in education. An area of interest I have always had, but did not have a name for until I was well into my teaching career, was the intense feelings my gifted and high ability students experienced. I would have one student crying when finding a dead insect on the playground. Another student would be able to read about a topic of interest while in class and look like he wasn't paying attention to the teacher (me) but actually be able to do both activities simultaneously.

I once observed a student who seemed so super charged that she never sat still and was always asking questions and moving on to the next concept before anyone else knew what had happened. As a child, I had an imaginary friend named Jane who could ask my Mom and Dad to do things that I had a problem asking them myself.

As an adult, I married a very gifted individual who never knew he had been identified. He only learned about himself when he was an adult, investigating the reasons he felt deeply about what was happening in the world as well as what was happening in our own neighborhood. I realized I needed to do some research to discover why the people in my life ... my students, my husband, and even in myself ... experienced the intensities I had identified in my classrooms and at home as a child and as an adult.

I first read the work of Kazimierz Dabrowski (1902-1980) whose research provided a lens through which I could start to understand these unique and intense characteristics. Dabrowski was a psychiatrist and psychologist from Poland who developed a theory that these intensities were actually necessary to experience advanced thinking. He also concluded that giftedness combined with five intensities (emotional, intellectual, imaginational, sensual, and psychomotor) were what led to higher-level development. He found that individuals may exhibit one or several of these intensities. "One who manifests several forms of over excitability sees reality in a different, stronger and more multi-sided manner."(Dabrowski, 1972, p. 7.)

Experiencing the world to an intense degree can be both joyful and frustrating. The joys and positive aspects of these intensities need to be highlighted and celebrated. Frustrations can be positively dealt with and used to help facilitate growth. Subsequently, I found and read a book by Brené Brown entitled Gifts of Imperfection. It was the subtitle of the book that really caught my eye: Let Go of Who You Think You're Supposed to Be and Embrace Who You Are. So often we have a vision of who we – or others – think we should be. Maybe others think we should not be so sensitive, not so buried in the text of a book where the focus is our passion, and not so immersed in daydreams. But maybe that is exactly who we are and what makes us unique.

Regardless of what others or our self-talk may be telling

us, as Arthur William Edgar O'Shaughnessy wrote in his ode:

"We are the music makers,
And we are the dreamers of dreams…
Yet we are the movers and shakers
Of the world for ever, it seems."

Last but not least, I became aware of Leslie Sword who is the Director of Gifted & Creative Services in Australia. She is a consultant who specializes in the psychology of the gifted and has worked with gifted people of all ages. She states, "If emotional intensity is seen and presented positively to gifted children as a strength, they can be helped to understand and value the gift of emotion. In this way gifted children will be empowered to express their unique selves in the world and use their gifts and talents with confidence and joy." Their mission statement caught my eye as well as my heart:

"GIFTED & CREATIVE Services is dedicated to providing information and services that encompass and nourish the whole gifted person and meet emotional, intellectual, physical and educational needs. Since our inception in 1979, our focus has been on all aspects of giftedness. We know about emotional issues, intensity, sensitivity, perfectionism, and the very real needs of visual-spatial learners. We know how unique gifted individuals tend to be when it comes to learning style and self-expression."

I was sold. I needed to find resources and texts for my students to help them bring out their positive benefits as well as deal with any negatives. In my attempt to find resources for my students, I found many articles written for teachers, but I did not find any of the positive presentations Leslie Sword referenced. I looked for books for children and again did not find what I envisioned. There are many books for children to help them deal with sensory disorders. That is not how intensities – or Sensational Sensibilities- should be framed.

So I decided to start by creating a card game using the five heightened senses that Dabrowski originally linked to gifted individuals. Then I shared my idea with students and teachers; they all encouraged me to write a guide to go along with my card game. Here it is. I hope you enjoy learning about your intensities or Sensational Sensibilities by reading this guide and playing the card games.

~ Patricia Farrenkopf ~

The creative instinct is, in its final analysis and in its simplest terms, an enormous extra vitality, a super-energy, born inexplicably in an individual, a vitality great beyond all the needs of his own living - an energy which no single life can consume. This energy consumes itself then in creating more life, in the form of music, painting, writing, or whatever is its most natural medium of expression. Nor can the individual keep himself from this process, because only by its full function is he relieved of the burden of this extra and peculiar energy - an energy at once physical and mental, so that all his senses are more alert and more profound than another man's, and all his brain more sensitive and quickened to that which his senses reveal to him in such abundance that actuality overflows into imagination. It is a process proceeding from within. It is the heightened activity of every cell of his being, which sweeps not only himself, but all human life about him, or in him, in his dreams, into the circle of its activity.

Pearl S. Buck

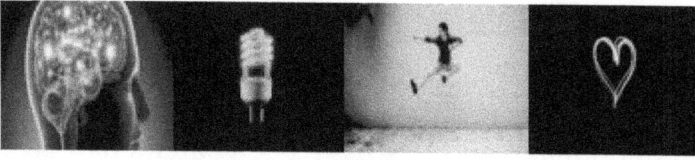

Chapter One
The Sensational Sensibilities

If you are reading this book, you may have been identified as a gifted and/or high ability individual. You may also have asked the question, "So what does being gifted and high ability really mean?"

It all begins when parents, teachers, and children/teens notice that they see you or recognize themselves experiencing the world differently. That does not mean that gifted and high ability people are better – it just means they are ... different. Sometimes this uniqueness is noticed at a young age. Maybe you started talking in sentences when you were age one. Maybe you read your first book when you were in preschool. Maybe you were older when you noticed that many of the new concepts in school were not new to you at all. Maybe you discovered an orchestra or band interest and were able to pick up any instrument and play it without first having lessons. Maybe you have always been able to see the multiple possibilities to solving a problem instead of using "the one right answer." Maybe you heard an event described by a classmate or a speaker as new and realized that you had insight into that experience all along.

You can see that there are variables to being gifted and thinking in a different manner. Variable is not just a mathematical term but explains why gifted and high ability individuals are more different from each other than they are alike. You can be young when identified, older when you are identified, and believe it or not, even an adult when you finally find out why you think and operate differently from other people. Your gift and ability can be one of general intellect or specific abilities in a school subject. You might be a budding thespian, dancer, artist, or musician. You might even have created an invention that could – or has – been patented. It is quite possible that many of your friends are also gifted.

Aristotle, an ancient Greek Philosopher, once said, "A friend is a second self, so that our consciousness of a friend's existence...makes us more fully conscious of our own existence." Translation: "What is a friend? It is another I." If you think about it, that makes a lot of sense. We look for friends whose interests are similar to ours. We seek someone to go to the movies with who likes fantasy movies as much as we do. Aristotle also said, "Knowing yourself is the beginning of wisdom." Knowing yourself includes being tuned in to the unique ways you experience life. You may actually have Sensational Sensibilities or have a friend who does. These Sensational Sensibilities cause you to experience life in 3D and Technicolor with Surround Sound. It can be pretty intense and that is good - you just need to know that it can be intense and be good at the same time! Not everyone will understand what you are experiencing. Sometimes when people do not understand, they react in a teasing or critical way.

The purpose of this book and accompanying deck of cards is to aid you in examining these Sensational Sensibilities. Let's start by looking at a paragraph explanation of each of the five sensibilities– with accompanying quotes from Aristotle.

Awarenesses
"Pleasure in the job puts perfection in the work."

Those who experience the Awareness Sensational Sensibility really appreciate certain sights, smells, tastes, and touches. Their life experience with these sensations is much more intense than experienced by many people. Some of their early reactions to input to the senses can be described as sheer delight. There may be other experiences that are avoided like with tags in clothing that may be extremely irritating. Nothing wrong with that – just remove the tags.

Imagining
"Thinking is different from perceiving and is held to be in part imagination, in part judgment."

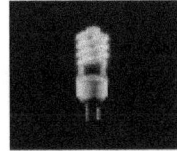

Those who experience the Imagining Sensational Sensibility are very playful with images and language. Their intricate ability to visualize and have elaborate dreams that they can remember leads to their ability to invent and fantasize. Your best classes are the ones where you can use your imagination. You may have even had an imaginary friend as a child. You have incredible ideas and need outlets such as writing and the arts to channel this Sensational Sensibility.

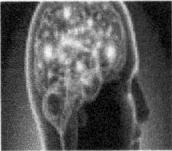

Thinking
"It is the mark of an educated mind to be able to entertain a thought without accepting it."

Those who experience the Thinking Sensational Sensibility really have the need to understand truth. They have a drive to constantly learn, and analyze and synthesize that learning. Their minds are always going at lightning speed, observing everything around them because they are by nature very curious. Concentration for long periods of time is not a problem, especially if it is during solving a problem in which they are passionately interested. They actually enjoy planning independently. Sensational thinkers are really focused on moral and ethical issues and fairness.

Energetic
"The energy or active exercise of the mind constitutes life."

Those who experience the Energetic Sensational Sensibility are constantly moving and seem to have unlimited energy. They can speak for extended lengths of time and at a very fast pace. They are enthusiastic organizers and like competitive activities. They have considerable drive. They have no problem with their constant movement.

Feelings
"Educating the mind without educating the heart is no education at all.

Those who experience the Feelings Sensational Sensibility have the remarkable ability to develop very close and deep relationships. Those with this sensibility demonstrate powerful and sustained attachments to people, places, and things. Compassion, empathy, and sensitivity are synonymous with their reactions to life experiences. These individuals are also extremely cognizant of their own feelings and how they are constantly growing and changing. You might have a thought that you are just overreacting; really you are really simply showing that you feel deeply.

Now it is time to consider each of these
Sensational Sensibilities
in more depth and detail...
and find out which ones are residing within
YOU.

The emotions are sometimes so strong that I work without knowing it. The strokes come like speech.

Vincent Van Gogh, painter

Chapter Two
Awarenesses

In all things of nature there is something of the marvelous. - Aristotle

What does it mean to have a Sensational Sensibility of Awareness? What is good about having an Awareness Sensational Sensibility?

Awarenesses Sensational Sensibility individuals don't just have some favorite things in their lives – those things are FAVORITES!!!!

They are obsessed with their interests in objects, the arts, and books. This heightened experience can be something pleasurable or not so pleasurable and be picked up from any one of the senses. When there is a displeasure picked up by the senses, those with this sensibility will only wear certain brands of socks, shirts without tags, and may avoid certain foods and things that have a smell.

There are many positives with being aware, as Jade Rivera points out. She refers to those with awareness sensational sensibilities as "our future taste makers and aesthetes." She has even identified some famous people who "have successfully harnessed" this sensibility:

Sofia Coppola:
American screenwriter,
director, producer

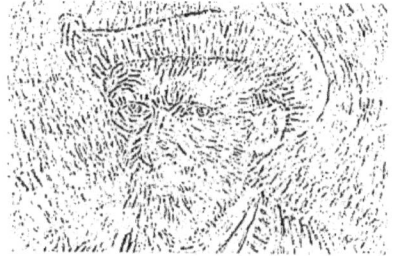

Vincent Van Gogh:
Dutch post-Impressionist painter

Jackie Kennedy:
First Lady to President John F. Kennedy
and fashion icon

Mark Morris:
American dancer, choreographer
and director

Ms. Rivera also asks the very important question, "What would the world have done without these great, gifted people? Can you imagine the bullying Mark Morris would go through in today's traditional school? Vincent Van Gogh never felt acceptance for his tremendous gifts, and we all know how that story ends."

Accept and appreciate
your
Awarenesses
Sensational Sensibility!!!

The Sensational Sensibility of Awareness includes the following
descriptions:

Notices texture of foods
Notices aromas
Notices nuances in tastes
Appreciates the beauty in writing, music, and art
Appreciates the beauty in nature
Notices beauty in objects, like jewelry
Sensitive to pollution
Sensitive to tags in clothing
Needs contentment
Prefers peacefulness

Now let's take those 10 Awareness Sensational Sensibility
descriptions and have a closer look.

Awarenesses | **Sensitive to Textures of Foods**

Notices texture of foods

Kendra Pierre-Louis writes about having sensitivity to food texture. She is happy that there is a new type of scientist researching the ways to make these textures palatable. Food sensory researchers from The Understanding & Insight Group, a consortium of scientists from the U.S. and New Zealand, have broken chewing preferences into four categories. Chewers like the foods you can chew for a long time, like gummy candy. Crunchers like foods that crunch, like potato chips. Suckers prefer foods that dissolve over time, like hard candies. Smooshers, prefer soft creamy foods, like puddings. The ultimate goal is to make all foods in different forms so they can be selected depending upon the texture of choice - so they can be smooshed, sucked, crunched, and / or chewed.

Awarenesses | **Sensitive to Smells**

Notices aromas

Phylameana lila Desy writes about her own ideas, and those of her readers, how to live in a world full of perfumes and toxic chemical smells. Most of her readers label themselves as having a "smeller that is way too sensitive." One reader shares that she rarely wears perfumes because they smell like bug repellent to her. Her readers not only share stories of their sensitivities but also strategies for coping:

- Avoiding anything advertised as having an artificial scent.
- Opening windows when possible to air out room then turn on air conditioner.

- Fighting unfriendly aromas with friendly ones – like orange.
- Chewing pieces of gum, inhaling through mouth and exhaling through nose.
- Using a saline nasal spray.
- Purchasing chemical free products for the home.
- Using a dehumidifier with HEPA filters

Awarenesses | **Sensitive to Tastes**

Notices tastes

Just as with textures, those with awarenesses sensibilities can be sensitive to tastes. As noted earlier, Jade Rivera points out that these sensitivities can lead to scientists who research ways to make foods palatable – both in texture and in taste.

Awarenesses | **Appreciates Beauty in Writing, Music, Art**

Notices the Beautiful World of the Arts

Have you ever experienced "getting lost" when listening to a piece of music, reading a piece of literature, or viewing a piece of art? Have you experienced becoming emotional when reading an excellent piece of literature? Have you cried when hearing a symphony play a particular favorite piece? Have you been able to see yourself in a piece of art as one of the characters? This is uniquely a human characteristic, to both create and appreciate beauty in art forms including literature. Those with this Sensational Sensibility can have a very intense reaction to viewing, reading, and listening to these art forms.

Awarenesses | **Appreciates Beauty in Nature**

Notices the Beautiful World of Nature

John Haltiwanger in a May 6, 2015 LIFE magazine article, "People Who Appreciate Nature Are Happier, Healthier And More Innovative" pointed to this appreciation as strength. It provides an experience of peaceful awareness that is hard to replicate. This can be a challenge due to the development of our cities as void of nature except for the man-made parks. He points out that John Muir, American naturalist, author, environmental philosopher, glaciologist and early advocate for the preservation of wilderness in the United States, once said,

"Going to the woods is going home; for I suppose we came from the woods originally."

Research has shown that people who not only appreciate nature but intentionally carve out time to spend time in it, are happier, healthier, and more creative. Nature reduces stress and helps us find meaning. Humans were never meant to be confined by concrete and steel 100 percent of the time. When we spend time in nature, we are reminded that all living organisms are connected. Nature strengthens our immune systems and our muscles. Chemicals given off by plants are called phytoncides, or wood essential oils. These oils strengthen the immune systems of humans when they are exposed to them. They even protect the plants that give them off from rotting.

Researchers have also discovered that inhaling these oils increases the number of natural kill cells in our bodies, which is a type of white blood cell. These kill cells are essential to the immune system, hunting and killing tumors or those cells infected. Haltiwanger observes that a walk in nature could end up saving your life. Other benefits include exercise through hiking in nature, which burns calories, strengthens the heart muscle, and helps to keep us fit. Hiking also provides quite a beautiful view of our world. Our minds become sharper and more inventive after spending time in nature. Often cell phones do not work on a hike, so that gives us an opportunity to get away from them and allow our minds to uncomplicate and become more intuitive and creative.

As Anne Frank once wrote,

"The best remedy for those who are afraid, lonely or unhappy is to go outside...
I firmly believe that nature brings solace in all troubles."

Awarenesses | **Loves objects that are beautiful, such as jewelry**

Notices beauty in objects, like jewelry

Just as with appreciating writing, music, and art, loving beautiful objects such as jewelry can be very descriptive of you. You have the ability to pair complimentary objects - for your pleasure as well as for others.

Awarenesses | **Sensitive to Pollution**

Air Quality Sensibility

Pollution is a world issue and problem to be solved. If you have a sensory reaction to pollution, you will most likely become a strong advocate for solving this problem. Something this important and understood to you could inspire you to work for a solution.

Awarenesses | **Sensitive to Tags in Clothing**

Skin Sensitivity

Does it bother you when you buy a new shirt and the tag in the back rubs against your skin? You are not alone! Two things to keep in mind. One – you can remove the tags from clothing very easily. Two – many new styles of clothing are created without tags but have information stamped on the inside of the piece. There are a multitude of style options of clothing to make it easy to avoid the skin sensitivities.

Awarenesses | **Need for Contentment**

Seeking Serenity

Contentment is being in a state of happiness and satisfaction. It is a state of mind. You can be in the driver's seat. It is not all about material possessions as in how much we have or how little. It is all about finding that place inside us, allowing a quiet contentment whatever else might be going on. It means being at peace with who we are. Experiencing contentment can start by taking a breath in, and deciding to release everything that makes us feel anxious and dissatisfied as we breathe out. Try settling deeply and quietly in a traffic jam, in the middle of an argument, or when tears are close. Let the commotion of the world simply come to rest. When we are able to live in that moment, we learn to accept and be in control. Our world can be very rushed and complicated. Contentment allows us to not just rush forward without a plan. We can instead direct our energy in the very best manner.

Awarenesses | **Need for Peacefulness**

Prefers tranquility

According to author Remez Sasson, there is inner peace and then there is outer peace. Inner peace is being at peace mentally, knowing that it is important to stay strong through trouble and stress. Inner peace is the opposite of inner stress or anxiousness. Focusing on this builds strength and confidence. Waiting to find outer peace, or stress free situations, should not be a prerequisite for inner peace. Use of affirmations, visualization, yoga, and meditation can be helpful in building this inner peace. It does take time and does not happen overnight. Be kind and patient with yourself.

Chapter Three
Energetic

The energy or active exercise of the mind constitutes life. - Aristotle

**What does it mean to have an Energetic Sensibility?
What is good about being an Energetic SS?**

The Energetic Sensational Sensibility is a heightened excitability
of the neuromuscular system.

The neuromuscular system includes all the muscles
in the body and the nerves controlling them. Every time you
move, communication between the brain and the muscles
is necessary. The nervous system provides the link between
thoughts and actions by sending messages that travel so fast
you don't even know it has happened. So nerves and muscles
also work together to make your body move as you wish. They
also make sure you do things you don't even think about, such
as breathing.

This Energetic Sensibility means you are always active
and energetic. Those with this sensibility love movement just
because it is movement. They demonstrate an abundance
of energy through rapid speech, being overwhelmingly
enthusiastic, working and playing hard, and just simply
needing action. When also feeling very emotional and tense,
they may talk and act compulsively, display nervous habits,

demonstrate a driven need to work or hyper-organize, or become incredibly competitive. They possess boundless physical and verbal energy which is transformed into seemingly endless activity. It is important for those individuals to build activity and movement into life and provide time for spontaneity and open-ended activities.

The Sensational Sensibility of Energy includes the following descriptions:

Rapid speech
Ability to be spontaneous
Enjoys competitions
Enthusiastic conversationalist
Ability to organize
Has established habits
Prefers fast action
Prefers fast moving sports
Physically expresses emotions
Can have trouble falling asleep at first

Now let's take those 10 Energetic Sensational Sensibility descriptions and have a closer look.

Energetic | **Speaks Quickly**

Rapid speech

When excited or overwhelmed, talking can become very fast and also louder. In a 1976 psychological study conducted by Norman Miller, this researcher found that at 195 words per minute, about the fastest that people speak in normal conversation, the message becomes more credible to those listening, and therefore more persuasive. Talking fast seems to signal confidence, intelligence, objectivity and superior knowledge. Going at about 100 words per minute, the usual lower limit of normal conversation, is associated with all the reverse attributes.

By the 1980s, research was showing that the effects of talking fast were not all positive. Researchers found that when someone talks quickly it can be hard to keep up with what they are saying, so the persuasive message doesn't have a chance to take hold. Smith and Shaffer in a 1991 study found that when a spoken message is counter-attitudinal, fast talking is more persuasive than when spoken at an intermediate rate of speed, with slow talking being the least persuasive of all. Conclusion: don't worry about your rate of speed of talking unless you want to make sure those listening understand what you are talking about.

Energetic | **Spontaneous**

Ability to be spontaneous

It is important to provide time to just be spontaneous. Much of life is scheduled and scripted out of need, but it is possible to reserve time for spontaneous activities. Spontaneity keeps your mind sharp. Having unknowns in your schedule and being comfortable with that can force you to really focus on what is also not spontaneous and necessary to do. The better you are at coping with unknown situations, the less stress you'll experience throughout the day. Feeling like the only choice you have in your day is having another glass of milk with your toast in the morning is really boring. Do something completely unexpected. Shake things up a bit. The spur-of-the-moment has a strange ability to lift a boring activity.

Energetic | **Enjoys Competitions**

Enjoys competitions

Healthy competition inspires us to do our best – not just good enough. When we compete we become more inquisitive, research independently, and learn to work with others. We strive to do more than is required. These abilities prepare children for future situations of all kinds. Whether it's applying to a special program or after school job or seeking recognition for a problem solved a new way, the ability to be competitive gives us an important edge. Competition can be healthy when it provides feedback to us about our performance and improvement, when winning is not the sole or primary objective, and when we get to learn about ourselves under challenging situations. Under these circumstances, competition can teach us invaluable lessons not typically learned in the classroom. Life requires risk taking on a daily basis. Competition provides practice in critical thinking, decision-making and problem solving.

Energetic | **Enthusiastic Conversationalist**

Enthusiastic conversationalist

You have much to share and enjoy conversations. Conversations indicate more than one person is talking.

It is good to remember these points to have even better conversations. Make sure you always include asking questions of the person with whom you are talking. Listen first to understand and then to respond. Pay sincere compliments. Be ready to comment with questions, ideas, facts and opinions on the issues in which other people are interested. Be humorous and laugh at other people's funny stories, even if you have heard them before, and without giving away someone else's punch line.

Energetic | **Extremely Organized**

Ability to organize

There are many benefits about being organized. If you have friends who are not that organized, your interest and ability to be extremely organized may be irritating to them. It is important to remember that nothing is perfect. Give yourself a break from organizing if it is cutting into your time to do other activities.

Energetic | **Established Habits**

Has established habits

We are creatures of habit. Benjamin Franklin once said that "your net worth to the world is usually determined by what remains after your bad habits are subtracted from your good ones." Actively and consciously building a daily routine for you instills plenty of good habits. When we consciously decide what we want to do with every day of our lives, we generally want to do what makes us happy or what gives us the most use. We build tons of good habits along the way by actively paying attention in our daily lives.

Positives include: saves work on the back end if you do a little each day, helps you become good at things, increases efficiency, don't have problems with willpower and motivation, and builds momentum as in saving $1 a day for 30 days to buy the shirt you want.

Energetic | **Prefers Fast Action**

Prefers fast action

You will probably never have a concern about weighing too much because you are always moving fast and burning calories. It is important to think about safety as you are buzzing around…and nutrition to supply the fuel to keep it up.

Energetic | **Prefers Fast Sports**

Prefers fast moving sports

What is the fastest moving sport? Would you believe badminton? Yes, the game that is considered a children's summer picnic activity is a much more serious game in many parts of the world such as Asia and is really the fastest sport of all. The shuttlecock has been measured as traveling as fast as 206 mph at the point of being hit. That is much faster than baseballs, cricket balls, hockey pucks, and golf balls.

Energetic | **Physically Expresses Emotions**

Physically expresses emotions

First, it is good to be aware of how you physically express emotions. If you can catch yourself hunching your shoulders, clenching your jaw, if you notice your chest tightening or perspiration forming on your brow, not only can you release the tension in areas you have muscle control over, but you can also take some time to mindfully become more aware of what it is you are feeling in the moment, giving these feelings the chance to tell you their important message. Many of us carry a lot of tension in our bodies and we are not even aware of it. Just the act of consciously releasing all this tension can do wonders for you because you are telling your brain that you are calm and relaxed, which in turn will make it cut down on producing harmful stress hormones. The better you feel the better your body feels, and the better your body feels the better you feel. This is of course because you are your body.

Energetic | May Have Trouble Falling Asleep

Can have trouble falling asleep at first

If you are an active person, it is difficult to just turn that energy off at night in order to sleep. It is literally difficult to quiet your mind. D.F.Bruce in WebMD suggests trying some of these tips for a better night's sleep.

Try…
- Making your bedroom a quiet place
- Taking a hot shower and sleeping in a cool room
- Adding shades to your windows or wear a sleep mask
- Trying soft music or Yoga before bedtime
- Getting extra rest if you are ill
- Eating a high carb snack before bedtime
- Aromatherapy
- Drinking chamomile or valerian herbal teas

Chapter Four
Feelings

Educating the mind without educating the heart is no education at all.
- Aristotle

What does it mean to feel deeply?
What is good about feeling deeply?
What makes us human?

One characteristic that makes humans who they are is feelings. There are highs and lows of our feelings.

Sometimes you may feel really great and the next minute you may be very sad and teary. These shifts are absolutely okay and are part of the human experience. As a gifted individual, this may be a sensational sensibility for you. That means that you can feel happiness and sadness in an intense way. You may "wear your heart on your sleeve" which is a saying that means your facial expressions or physical reactions to those highs and lows can be seen by others and you can also feel those inside you.

Being aware of your intense feelings will help you realize what you need and want. It helps you build close relationships. Being aware of the intensity and duration (length of time it lasts) of your super sensibility emotions can help you describe your feelings with clarity and address possible confusion, all while moving through intense feelings in a positive way.

The Feeling Sensational Sensibility includes
the following descriptions:

Sense of Responsibility
Need to Always Do Better
Shyness
Concern for Others
Heightened Sense of Right and Wrong
Strong Memories of Feelings
Feeling You Should Be Able to Do Something
about a Problem
Being Uncomfortable with Change
Need for Security
Physical Response to Emotions

Now let's take those 10 Feeling Sensational Sensibility
descriptions and have a closer look.

Feelings | **Sense of Responsibility**

Sense of Responsibility

Being responsible is definitely a good thing. It is an essential characteristic in living life.. There are some tasks we must do alone; some we can do in pairs, some in groups, and so on. Sometimes our intense emotions can make us feel responsible for things that we are not at all responsible for doing. Have you ever had the experience of being in a classroom where the teacher has to tell the class they are too loud? Have you ever felt responsible, even if you were perfectly quiet at that moment?

Feelings | **Sense of Needing to Do Better**

Sense of Needing to Do Better

Improvement is also a good thing. All of us, at any age, can learn new concepts that improve our understanding. It is important to remember that improving is not synonymous with being perfect. Humans learn through trying to solve problems that don't work the first time, the second time, or maybe even after more attempts. We do keep getting closer to solutions by finding out what does not work. If you never had this experience of an attempt not working, you may even be trying things that were way too easy for you.

Feelings | **Sometimes Shy**

Sense of Shyness

By some estimates, 40% of the human population is shy. Some research also points out the positives of being shy.

Shy people are often very deep thinkers, extremely observant, and purposeful listeners. Sometimes shy people have just not found others who are similar to them so it may feel uncomfortable making friends. Remember what Socrates said about friends: "A friend is another 'I'."

Feelings | **Shows Concern for Others**

Sense of Showing Concern for Others

Another word for showing concern for others is empathy. Empathy is different from sympathy. Empathy is actually being able to experience the feelings of someone else. Sympathy is when you care about and can understand that someone is having a hard time. Those who have empathy are often the change agents in our world who see a situation of concern and act to make it better.

Feelings | **Heightened Sense of Right and Wrong**

Heightened Sense of right and wrong

Do some of the following scenarios sound familiar? Have you ever told the truth even when you knew you would be the one getting into trouble? Have you made it a point to make friends with classmates who have no other friends? Has someone acted in a bad manner toward you and you forgave them, giving them another chance because everyone can make a mistake? You are demonstrating a heightened sense of right and wrong. Another word synonymous with this sensibility is integrity.

Feelings | **Strong Memory of Feelings**

Super Sense of Strong memory of feelings

Many people remember events from their past experiences. Possessing a Feeling Sensational Sensibility can make it possible for you to remember these moments through how you felt at the moment it happened. You can actually break out in a sweat just by remembering an anxious event from your past.

Feelings | **Sometimes Feeling You Should Be Able to Do Something You Cannot**

Sense of feeling like you should be able to do something about a situation that may be out of your control

You know there are problems in the world such as hunger, war, lack of fresh water...and you cannot solve those problems immediately. Sometimes just making a dent in the problem is just the contribution needed to start others to think about how they can take part in solving a really big problem.

Feelings | **Changes Can Be Difficult at First**

May not be super comfortable with changes at first

Someone once said, "Change is hard – why don't you go first?" Change is inevitable. We all go through changes as we age. Some changes are not as gradual, like if a parent is transferred to a new city because of his/her job. Dealing with both types of changes takes time and it is okay not to not feel comfortable especially at first. It is important to realize that change is not like turning a switch from off to on. The change has stages and your comfort level does as well. Looking for the positives that might come from that change is a great way to deal with the stress that comes with any change, especially if you have an emotion Sensational Sensibility.

Feelings | **Need to Feel Secure**

Desire to feel secure

All of us need to feel safe. On Maslow's Hierarchy of Needs, safety is only second to breathing! There are many definitions of safe. You need to feel physically safe by having a home and caring adults in your life to help you as you grow up. It is important to feel safe with friends and other relationships so that you are able to share your thoughts without being judged. It is true that people may have many acquaintances but a few real friends. Those friends are the ones who are very similar to you in some ways and also need that safe and secure relationship so they can share their feelings with you without judgment.

Feelings | **Physical Response to Emotions**

May show/feel your emotions – blush, butterflies in stomach, etc.

Sensational Sensibility emotions can be really strong. Everyone has some degree of physical reaction to being anxious, but super sense emotions can be really intense. For those butterflies, try chewing gum if you do not feel like eating. That sends a signal to your brain and actually relaxes you by the release of adrenalin.

Chapter Five
Imagining

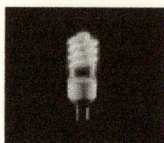

*Thinking is different from perceiving and is held
to be in part imagination, in part judgment.
-Aristotle*

**What does it mean to be Sensational Imaginer? What is good
about being an Sensational Sensibility Imaginer?**

Imagination involves both tangible and intangible features of
our experiences. Visualization involves the tangible features of
our experiences.

To provide an example, think about imagining you are in
a snow storm . You would be in the moment and taking in the
experience. Visualizing that same snow storm would involve
focusing on what your surroundings looked like while being
pelted with snow, ice, and wind. Albert Einstein even once said,
"Imagination is more important than knowledge. Knowledge
is limited. Imagination encircles the world." Imagery is a
special way to use your imagining Sensational Sensitivity.
One of the most powerful tools of imagery is using it to relax.
Imagery can be used like a mini getaway to deal with those
stressful situations we all experience. This is not avoiding the
situation but rather putting stress on hold by using imagery
to successfully deal with the stress you are experiencing.

Maintaining instead of draining your energy and your desired positive solution assists in coping with challenges.

Imagery has also been found to stimulate our immune systems, increasing or decreasing blood flow to areas of the human body and contributing to the healing process.

Like emotion, imagination makes us human. We are natural scenario builders and story tellers, and do so with the help of fantasy and our imagination. Songs have been sung, poems have been written, and problems have been solved through this imaginative, daydreaming play of thoughts.

The Sensational Sensibility of imagination includes the following descriptions:

Vivid Dreaming
Being Cautious of the Unknown
Good Sense of Humor
Magical thinker
Love poetry
Love music and dance
Prefer fantasy to non-fiction
Enjoy daydreaming
Had an imaginary friend when you were little
Ability to visualize in detail

Now let's take those 10 Imagination Sensational Sensibility descriptions and have a closer look.

Imagining | **Vivid Dreams**

You have vivid dreams

The Roman poet Lucretius from the first century B.C. was one of the first to detect REM or rapid eye movement when he observed one of his dogs twitching while sleeping by the fire. As Lucretius observed his dog's eyes dart back and forth beneath its closed eyelids, he noted, "the animal appeared to be chasing some type of phantom prey in its mind."

Today's scientists didn't connect the significance of REM sleep until the early 1950s. REM is the time frame of our sleep when most of our vivid dreams occur, rerunning the activities of the day through our dreams at night. Some people do not remember their dreams or have vague storylines attached to the reruns of their daily events. Those who are Sensational Sensibility Imaginers not only remember their dreams but have ones that are very vivid, sometimes even in color and with movie credits. They can relate their dream storyline in great detail and because their dreams seem real, they often need to take time to realize their dream was just that - a dream and not reality.

Imagining | **Cautious of the Unknown**

Cautious of the unknown

No one can argue effectively that it is not a good idea to be cautious. Especially when faced with a new challenge or situation, it is good to "tread lightly" or proceed carefully. If there is not forethought when faced with unknown conditions, actions can be dangerous and risky. Once the conditions are examined, good risks can be taken.

Imagining | **Good Sense of Humor**

Good sense of humor

A good sense of humor is a wonderful asset to have. Having a good sense of humor can help you work with and enjoy others, improve your general physical and emotional health, and even help deescalate difficult situations. Interestingly enough, you don't have to be funny to have a sense of humor. The most important requirement is your ability to see the multiple sides of any situation.

Imagining | **Magical Thinker**

Magical thinker

Arthur C. Clarke observed, "Any sufficiently advanced technology is indistinguishable from magic." Magical thinking, according to author Matthew Hutson of 7 Laws of Magical Thinking, is "Believing that positive thoughts work wonders, leading you to have more positive thoughts, bringing all those proven benefits of optimism and positive visualization." Hutson knows that beneficial magical thinking is not when you wear your lucky red socks to the baseball game or believe that buying a lucky four leaf clover from a salesman will bring you a fortune. William Arthur Ward's quote sums it up: "If you can imagine it, you can achieve it. If you can dream it, you can become it."

Imagining | **Love of Poetry**

Loves poetry

According to Dwight Longnecker of the Intercollegiate

Studies Institute in Wilmington, Delaware, there are three benefits of reading and writing poetry. First, it puts you in touch with your emotions. Second, you have to think creatively and in "mind bending" ways. Anything can happen in poetry, from using metaphors to express meaning to providing shock and awe in the last stanza. Last but not least, it stretches your imagination because you have to step out of the academic, literal world and see ideas from many different perspectives.

Imagining | Love of Music and Dance

Love music and dance

Music and dance are two forms of expression and many times are used simultaneously. According to Lin Marsh from the British Council Voices, as humans we are naturally creative, musical and artistic. When allowed to express emotions through music and dance, rather than dancing and using music from a scripted piece, we can become even more imaginative and self-aware. Global collaborations, using music and dance, can overcome any language or cultural barricade. Music and dance are both essential to our development as humans.

Imagining | Love of Fantasy

Prefer Fantasy to Non-Fiction

According to Professor John Stephens of Macquaire University in Sydney, Australia, fantasy is a genre of literature that allows the reader to experiment with different ways to see the world. Fantasy can take a completely hypothetical scenario and allow the reader to make connections between the fantasy and their own reality. Problem solving for our future definitely requires thinkers to see possibilities from different perspectives.

Nonfiction can provide the situation as it is while fantasy can provide a glimpse of what could be.

Imagining | **Love of Daydreaming**

Enjoy daydreaming

Daydreaming is misunderstood. Some think that daydreaming is a signal of a lazy person and takes us away from the really important thoughts of the day. According to Dr. Marcus Raichle, a neurologist and radiologist at Washington University, "When you don't use a muscle, that muscle really isn't doing much of anything... But when your brain is supposedly doing nothing and daydreaming, it's really doing a tremendous amount. We call it 'resting state,' but the brain isn't resting at all. When we float down our inner stream of consciousness our brains actually become highly stimulated, with many areas, including the pre-frontal lobe and executive center becoming active." So a quote from Langston Hughes to finish this paragraph on daydreaming: "Hold fast to dreams, for if dreams die, life is a broken-winged bird that cannot fly."

Imagining | **Had an Imaginary Friend as a Child**

Had an imaginary friend when you were little

According to Karen Stephens of The Parent Exchange, the play a child experiences with an imaginary friend is different from children acting out characters featured on TV shows or in movies. Familiar movie or cartoon characters might give the child an idea to start with for fantasy, but a true imaginary friend comes from a child's own mind. Their traits, emotions, and conversation all spring from the child's own perceptions.

Imagining | **Visualize in Detail**

Ability to visualize in detail

You don't have to see it to see it. That may not seem to make sense, but think about it. You can visualize what has not been created yet. It could be through a story, a poem, or even an invention. Sometimes it starts through vividly dreaming at night or daydreaming. You will be able to describe what you visualize through metaphors, bringing abstract meaning into clarity. In a way, your visualization explains your imagination. You have come full circle.

Chapter Six
Thinking

It is the mark of an educated mind to be able to entertain a thought without accepting it.
-Aristotle

What does it mean to be intellectual?
What is good about being intellectual?

Humans are naturally curious about almost everything. Our constant "why" questions really irritated our parents and teachers - at times. If we want to grow and improve, we need to ask questions. We need to be curious.

The Sensational Sensibility Thinker has a deep and complex drive to know. This drive does not stop at a surface level but in a sense actually peels back layers to truly understand an issue or concern.

There are always those extreme examples when too much curiosity is not good. Consider Isaac Newton. He actually once wedged a flat stick between his skull and the back of his eye, recording the visual experiences he had. He wanted to know how it was exactly that humans perceived color and light. When curiosity is tempered with some safety in mind, it can result in a great thinking experience.

The Sensational Sensibility of Thinking includes
the following descriptions:

Deeply curious
Love the idea of knowledge
Love the process of learning
Love the challenges of problem solving
Avid reader
Asks probing questions
Theoretical thinker
Analytical thinker
Independent thinker
Ability to concentrate for long periods of time

Now let's take those 10 Intellectual Sensational Sensitivity
descriptions and have a closer look.

Thinking | **Deep Curiosity**

Deeply curious

The level of curiosity for the Sensational Sensibility Thinker is described as insatiable.

According to Donald Latumahina, there are four benefits of curiosity. First, it makes your mind active instead of passive. Curious people are always asking questions and searching for answers in their minds. Since the mind is like a muscle that becomes stronger through constant exercise, this mental curiosity exercise makes your mind stronger.

Second, it makes your mind observant of new ideas. When you are curious about something, your mind expects and anticipates new ideas related to it. When the ideas come they will soon be recognized. Without curiosity, the ideas may pass right in front of you and yet you miss them because your mind is not prepared to recognize them. Just think, how many great ideas may have been lost due to lack of curiosity?

Third, it opens up new worlds and possibilities. By being curious you will be able to see new worlds and possibilities which are normally not visible. They are hidden behind the surface of normal life, and it takes a curious mind to look beneath the surface and discover these new worlds and possibilities.

Last but not least, it brings excitement into your life. The life of curious people is far from boring. It's neither dull nor routine. There are always new things that attract their attention; there are always new 'toys' to play with. Instead of being bored, curious people have an adventurous life. So it is important to keep an open mind, don't take anything for granted, ask questions relentlessly, and see learning as fun and never boring.

Thinking | **Love of Knowledge**

Love the idea of knowledge

The term for a person who loves seeking knowledge is a wonk. Another word used is a philosopher - philo (love) sophia (wisdom). Another relevant word here is autodidact. This is someone who is literally self-taught, but with a strong sense of one who has sought out knowledge rather than been instructed. Whether one is known as a philosopher, an autodidact, or a wonk, they are always thinking and questioning.

Thinking | **Love of Learning**

Love the process of learning

No matter what the environment or topic, the love of learning is present. Parents and teachers are always encouraging the development of a love of learning; in reality it really cannot be taught. It is created in an environment of support in which students can develop their own ideas, express feelings, take chances, make choices, share their opinions, and most of all, grow up to be strong individuals.

Thinking | **Love of Problem Solving**

Love the challenges of problem solving

The level of effort in problem solving is described as tenacious. Problem-solving is a mental process that involves discovering, analyzing and solving problems. The ultimate goal of problem-solving is to overcome obstacles and find a solution that best resolves the issue. The best strategy for solving a problem depends largely on the unique situation.

Problem solving requires two distinct types of mental skill: analytical and creative. Analytical or logical thinking includes skills such as ordering, comparing, contrasting, evaluating and selecting.

Thinking | **Love of Reading**

Avid reader – The level of love of reading is constant

According to the Pew Research Center (did you know Pew is a family name and not an acronym?), the typical person reads or listens to 4 books per year. The average for all people is 12 books per year.

That means a small number of people are reading a ton. Those people are known as avid readers, and there are a few things they do differently. They read more narrative writing, they frequent places to purchase books like bookstores and online book sellers, and they were early readers as children. They can also often read a book and pay attention simultaneously to another activity, such as a class or a movie on television.

Thinking | **Love of Asking Probing Questions**

Asks probing questions

The level of probing questions is described as endless. The types of questions fit into something called Socratic Questioning. Socrates was one of the greatest educators who taught by asking questions and thus drew out answers from his pupils ('ex duco', means to 'lead out', which is the root of 'education'). Sadly, he martyred himself by drinking hemlock rather than compromising his principles. That was a bold action, but not a good survival strategy. But then he lived very frugally and was known for his eccentricity. One of his pupils was Plato, who wrote up much of what we know of him. Socrates asked his pupils, probably often to their initial annoyance but more often to their ultimate delight, these types of questions: conceptual clarification, probing assumptions, probing rationale reasons and evidence, questioning viewpoints and perspectives, and probing implications and consequences. The overall purpose of Socratic questioning, is to challenge accuracy and completeness of thinking in a way that acts to move people toward their ultimate answer.

Thinking | **Love of Theory**

Theoretical thinker

A theory is an explanation of something. It is typically an explanation of a class of phenomena, rather than a single specific event. Instead of explaining why there is a brown stain on my tie, a theory would explain why men's ties often have brown stains.

Theories are often expressed as chains of causality: this happens because this and that happened just when something else happened and this in turn happened because ... you get the idea!

Thinking | **Love of Analysis**

Analytical thinker

Analytical thinking is a critical component of visual thinking that gives one the ability to solve problems quickly and effectively. It involves a methodical step-by-step approach to thinking that allows you to break down complex problems into single and manageable components.

Analytical thinking involves the process of gathering relevant information and identifying key issues related to this information. This type of thinking also requires you to compare sets of data from different sources, identify possible cause and effect patterns, and draw appropriate conclusions from these datasets in order to arrive at appropriate solutions. Analytical thinking can be broken down into three main steps: gather information, identify issues and problems, and organize the information.

Thinking | **Love of Independence**

Independent thinker

Independent thinkers feel the need to make sense of the world based on personal observations and experiences rather than just going along with the thoughts of others. That actually takes quite a bit of courage.

Thinking | **Love of Concentration**

Ability to concentrate for long periods of time

When you are really interested in a topic, it is possible to concentrate for extremely long periods of time. When you are not interested in a topic, it is more difficult to concentrate for long periods of time.

The music is not in the notes, but in the silence between.

Wolfgang Amadeus Mozart, musician

Chapter Seven
Games

You have a deck of 52 cards:

2 wild cards

5 suits:

10 Awareness Cards

10 Energetic Cards

10 Feelings Cards

10 Imagining Cards

10 Thinking Cards

(A, 2, 3, 4, 5, 6, 7, 8, 9, 10)

Sensational Sensibility Identity Game

1. Remove the wild cards from the Sensational Sensibility Card Deck.

2. Turn each of the remaining 50 Sensational Sensibility cards face up and one at a time.

3. Decide if the sense description REALLY describes YOU:

- If it does REALLY describe YOU, keep the card face up in front of you.

- If it KIND OF describes you, place the card in the holding pile.

- If it REALLY DOES NOT describe YOU, place in a discard pile.

4. Continue until you have gone through all of the cards.

5. Line up the cards you kept face up in front of you.

6. Reduce the cards or review the holding and then the discard pile further until you have a total of at most 11 cards left in front of you, discarding the cards that are the least like you as compared to the other cards.

Which Sensational Sensibilities do your 11 remaining cards represent?

Continuity Game

1. Remove wild cards.

2. Deal all the cards. Everyone need not have the same

number of cards if the deck doesn't divide evenly.

3. The person to the dealer's left makes the first play. This person takes the lowest card he has in a particular suit and plays it in the center of the table.

4. Play does not go around the circle after that.

5. The player who has the next-highest card in that suit plays it on top. And then the next highest card is played by whoever has it.

6. Play continues until the Ace (the highest card of the suit) is reached. The player who plays the Ace then plays the lowest card he has from a new suit and the process begins again.

7. The first player to get rid of all his cards wins the hand. The other players have points subtracted for the cards they have left. Keeping score is not essential.

Wild Card Game

1. Remove one wild card and leave one in the deck as the Wild Card.

2. Deal all the cards. Players sort through their cards, making as many pairs as possible, and placing these pairs face-up on the table in front of them.

3. Pairs can be made with A-10 numbers or suits. (a pair would be two 9s or 2 feeling cards)

4. Starting with the dealer, each player then takes a turn fanning out their hands so that the player to their left can draw one card. The player must not be allowed to see the player's hand from which they are drawing.

5. Play continues in this fashion. As players make pairs in their hand, they discard them immediately onto the table.

6. Each player is trying to get rid of his cards as fast as possible.
7. The player left holding the unmatched card, the Wild Card, loses that hand.

Reference List

Introduction

Brown, B. (2010). Gifts of Imperfection. Center City, MN: Hazeldon Publishing.

Dabrowski, K. (1972). Positive Disintegration. London: Gryf Publications.

Lind, S. (2011). Overexcitability and the Gifted. SENG. Retrieved from: http://sengifted.org/overexcitability-and-the-gifted/

Sword, L. (n.d.). Gifted and Creative. Retirieved from: http://giftedservices.com.au/aboutus.html

Chapter Two

Holmes, L. (2014). 9 Things Only Shy People Understand. Huffington Post. Retrieved from: http://www.huffingtonpost.com/2014/06/09/shy-people-annoyances_n_5352330.html

Kuzujanakis, M. (2016). The Intensities of Giftedness. Huffington Post.Retrieved from: http://www.huffingtonpost.com/ marianne-kuzujanakis/the-intensities-ofgifted_b_8134926.html

Chapter Three

Bruce, D.F. (n.d.). 8 EZZZZ Sleep Tips for Teens. WebMD. Retrieved from: http://teens.webmd.com/features/8-ezzz-sleep-tips-teens#1

Miller, N. (1976). Speed of Speech and Persuasion. Journal of Personality and Social Psychology, Vol 34(4), Oct 1976, 615-624.

Piechowski, M. (2014). Mellow Out They Say. Unionville, NY: Royal Fireworks Press.

Smith, S. & Schaffer, D. (1991). Celerity and Cajolery: Rapid Speech May Promote or Inhibit Persuasion through its Impact on Message Elaboration. Personality and Social Psychology. Retrieved from: http://journals.sagepub.com/doi/10.1177/0146167291176009

Wernick, A. (2015). The World's Fastest Sport Isn't the One You're Thinking Of. PRI – Science Friday. Retrieved from: https://www.pri.org/stories/2015-01-07/worlds-fastest-sport-isnt-one-youre-thinking

Chapter Four

Desy, P. (2016). Coping Strategies for Scent Sensitive Persons. Thought Co. Retrieved from: www.thoughtco.com/strategies-for-people-sensitive-to-smells-   1731104

Haltiwanger, J. (2015). People Who Appreciate Nature Are Happier, Healthier And More Innovative. Life Magazine. Retrieved from: http://elitedaily.com/life/people-who-appreciate-nature-are-happier-healthier-and-less-stressed/1024486/

Joyce, M.W. (2016). 6 Strategies to Finding Contentment in the Present. Huffington Post. Retrieved from: http://www.huffingtonpost.com/melissa-wilder- joyce/6-strategies-to-finding-contentment-in-the-present_b_10559632.html

Pierre-Louis, K. (2016). Texture is the Final Frontier of Food Science. Popular Science. Retrieved from: http://www.popsci.com/texture-food-Science

Rivera, J. (2014). How to Identify and Cope with Sensual Overexcitabilities. Educator Innovator. Retrieved from: http://www.jadeannrivera.com/how-to-identify-and-cope-with-overexcitabilities-part-5-of-5-sensual-overexcitability/

Sasson, R. (2017). The Benefits of Peace of Mind and Tranquility. Success Consciousness. Retrieved from:http://www. successconsciousness.com/peace_benefits.htm

Chapter Five

Jones, A.Z. (2016). What are Clark's Laws? Thought Company. Retrieved from: https://www.thoughtco.com/what-are-clarkes-laws-2699067

Lavers, C. (2016). The Psychological Benefits of Daydreaming. Wake Up World. Retrieved from: https://wakeup-world.com/2016/07/14/memory-focus-creativity-empathy-the-psychological-benefits-of-daydreaming/

Longnecker, D. (2014). Why You Need Poetry. Intercollegiate Studies. Retrieved from: https://home.isi.org/why-you-need-poetry

March, L. (2015). Why Song and Dance are Essential for Children's Development. British Council Voices. Retrieved from: https://www.britishcouncil.org/voices-magazine/why-song-and-dance-are-essential-development

Stephens, J. (2014). Children's Fantasy Literature: Why Escaping Reality is Good for Kids. The Conversation. Retrieved from: http://theconversation.com/childrens-fantasy-literature-why-escaping-reality-is-good-for-kids-22307

Stephens, K. (2007). Imaginary Friends. Parenting Exchange. Retrieved from: http://www.easternflorida.edu/community-resources/child-development-centers/parent-resource-library/documents/imaginary-friends.pdf

Chapter Six

Dhiman, G. (2015). What is the Word for One Who Loves to Learn? Knowledge Lover. Retrieved from: https://knowledgelover.com/word-for-someone-who-loves-to-learn/

Dow, P.E. (2013). Virtuous Minds: Intellectual Character Development. Downers Grove, IL: IVP Academic.

Kaye, S. & Thomson, P. (2007). Philosophy for Teens:Questioning Life's Big Ideas. Waco, TX: Prufrock Press.

Wittington, T. (2016). How Many Books Does the Average Person Read? Iris: Reading at the Speed of Thought. Retrieved from: https://www.irisreading.com/how-books-does-the-average-person-read/

Developing the Gifted Series

Order at www.fishtailpublishing.org

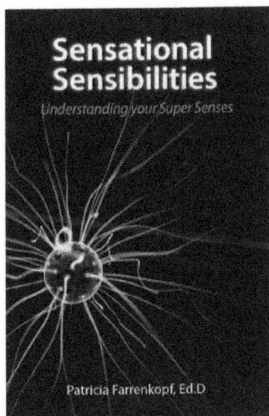

Volume 1

Sensational Sensibilities

Card deck available for purchase

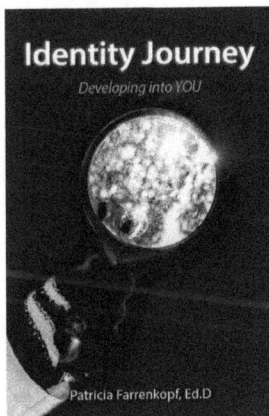

Volume 2

Identity Journey

Card deck and activity sheet available for purchase

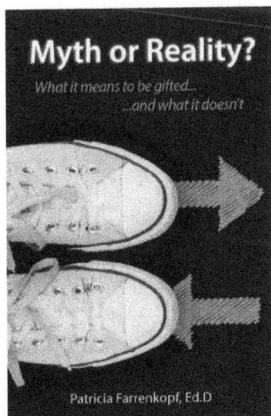

Volume 3

Myth or Reality?

Card deck available for purchase

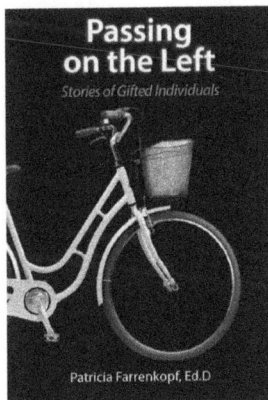

Volume 4

Passing on the Left

Card deck and activity sheet available for purchase

Fishtail Publishing

www.ingramcontent.com/pod-product-compliance
Lightning Source LLC
Chambersburg PA
CBHW021203090426
42740CB00008B/1217